CONGREGATION FOR CATHOLIC EDUCATION
(FOR EDUCATIONAL INSTITUTIONS)

# "MALE AND FEMALE HE CREATED THEM"

TOWARDS A PATH OF DIALOGUE
ON THE QUESTION OF
GENDER THEORY IN EDUCATION

*All documents are published
thanks to the generosity of the supporters
of the Catholic Truth Society*

# CONTENTS

INTRODUCTION . . . . . . . . . . . . . . . . . . . . . . . . . . . . . . 3

LISTENING. . . . . . . . . . . . . . . . . . . . . . . . . . . . . . . . . . . 7
   Brief Overview . . . . . . . . . . . . . . . . . . . . . . . . . . . . . . 7
   Points of Agreement . . . . . . . . . . . . . . . . . . . . . . . . . . 9
   Critique . . . . . . . . . . . . . . . . . . . . . . . . . . . . . . . . . . . 11

REASONING. . . . . . . . . . . . . . . . . . . . . . . . . . . . . . . . . 14
   Rational Arguments. . . . . . . . . . . . . . . . . . . . . . . . . . . 14

PROPOSING. . . . . . . . . . . . . . . . . . . . . . . . . . . . . . . . 17
   Christian Anthropology. . . . . . . . . . . . . . . . . . . . . . . . 17
   The Family . . . . . . . . . . . . . . . . . . . . . . . . . . . . . . . . 20
   The School . . . . . . . . . . . . . . . . . . . . . . . . . . . . . . . . 22
   Society. . . . . . . . . . . . . . . . . . . . . . . . . . . . . . . . . . . . 24
   Forming Formators . . . . . . . . . . . . . . . . . . . . . . . . . . 25

CONCLUSIONS . . . . . . . . . . . . . . . . . . . . . . . . . . . . . 29

*First published 2019 by The Incorporated Catholic Truth Society 42-46 Harleyford Road London SE11 5AY. Libreria Editrice Vaticana omnia sibi vindicat iura. Sine eiusdem licentia scripto data nemini liceat hunc textum denuo imprimere aut in aliam linguam vertere. Copyright © 2019 Libreria Editrice Vaticana, Città del Vaticano. This edition © 2019 The Incorporated Catholic Truth Society.*
*ISBN 978 1 78469 620 7*

# INTRODUCTION

1. It is becoming increasingly clear that we are now facing what might accurately be called an *educational crisis*, especially in the field of affectivity and sexuality. In many places, curricula are being planned and implemented which "allegedly convey a neutral conception of the person and of life, yet in fact reflect an anthropology opposed to faith and to right reason".[1] The disorientation regarding anthropology which is a widespread feature of our cultural landscape has undoubtedly helped to destabilise the family as an institution, bringing with it a tendency to cancel out the differences between men and women, presenting them instead as merely the product of historical and cultural conditioning.

2. The context in which the *mission of education* is carried out is characterised by challenges emerging from varying forms of an ideology that is given the general name "gender theory", which "denies the difference and reciprocity in nature of a man and a woman and envisages a society without sexual differences, thereby eliminating the anthropological basis of the family. This ideology leads to educational programmes and legislative enactments that promote a personal identity and emotional intimacy radically separated from the biological difference between male and female. Consequently, human identity becomes the choice of the individual, one which can also change over time".[2]

3. It seems clear that this issue should not be looked at in isolation from the broader question of education in the call to love,[3] which

---

[1] BENEDICT XVI, *Address to Members of the Diplomatic Corps*, 10 January 2011.

[2] FRANCIS, Post-Synodal Apostolic Exhortation *Amoris Laetitia*, 19 March 2016, 56.

[3] Cf. JOHN PAUL II, Post-Synodal Apostolic Exhortation *Familiaris Consortio*, 22 November 1981, 6; Cf. JOHN PAUL II, Letter to Families *Gratissimam Sane*, 2 February 1994, 16; Cf. John Paul II, *General Audience*, 8 April 1981 in *Insegnamenti*, IV/1 (1981), pp. 903-908.

should offer, as the Second Vatican Council noted, "a positive and prudent education in sexuality" within the context of the inalienable right of all to receive "an education that is in keeping with their ultimate goal, their ability, their sex, and the culture and tradition of their country, and also in harmony with their fraternal association with other peoples in the fostering of true unity and peace on earth".[4] The Congregation for Catholic Education has already offered some reflections on this theme in the document "Educational Guidance in Human Love: Outlines for Sex Education".[5]

4. The Christian vision of anthropology sees sexuality as a fundamental component of one's personhood. It is one of its modes of being, of manifesting itself, communicating with others, and of feeling, expressing and living human love. Therefore, our sexuality plays an integral part in the development of our personality and in the process of its education: "In fact, it is from [their] sex that the human person receives the characteristics which, on the biological, psychological and spiritual levels, make that person a man or a woman, and thereby largely condition his or her progress towards maturity and insertion into society".[6] As each person grows, "such diversity, linked to the complementarity of the two sexes, allows a thorough response to the design of God according to the vocation to which each one is called".[7] In the light of this, "affective-sex education must consider the totality of the person and insist therefore on the integration of the biological, psycho-affective, social and spiritual elements".[8]

---

[4] SECOND VATICAN ECUMENICAL COUNCIL, Decl. On Christian Education, *Gravissimum Educationis*, 28 October 1965, 1.

[5] CONGREGATION FOR CATHOLIC EDUCATION, *Educational Guidance in Human Love, Outlines for Sex Education*, 1 November 1983.

[6] CONGREGATION FOR THE DOCTRINE OF THE FAITH, *Persona Humana, Declaration on Certain Questions Concerning Sexual Ethics,* 29 December 1975, 1.

[7] *Educational Guidance in Human Love, Outlines for Sex Education*, 5.

[8] *Ibid.,* 35.

5. The Congregation for Catholic Education, as part of its remit, wishes to offer in this document some reflections which, it is hoped, can guide and support those who work in the education of young people, so as to help them address in a methodical way (and in the light of the universal vocation to love of the human person) the most debated questions around human sexuality.[9] The methodology in mind is based on three guiding principles seen as best suited to meet the needs of both individuals and communities: to *listen*, to *reason* and to *propose*. In fact, listening carefully to the needs of the other, combined with an understanding of the true diversity of conditions, can lead to a shared set of rational elements in an argument, and can prepare one for a Christian education rooted in faith that "throws a new light on everything, manifests God's design for man's total vocation, and thus directs the mind to solutions which are fully human".[10]

6. If we wish to take an approach to the question of gender theory that is based on the path of dialogue, it is vital to bear in mind the distinction between the ideology of gender on the one hand, and the whole field of research on gender that the human sciences have undertaken on the other. While the ideologies of gender claim to respond, as Pope Francis has indicated, "to what are at times understandable aspirations", they also seek "to assert themselves as absolute and unquestionable, even dictating how children should be raised",[11] and thus preclude dialogue. However, other work on gender has been carried out which tries instead to achieve a deeper understanding of the ways in which sexual difference between men and women is lived out in a variety of cultures. It is in relation to this type of research that we should be open to listen, to reason and to propose.

---

[9] Cf. *Ibid.*, 21-47, in which the Christian vision of sexuality is set out.
[10] SECOND VATICAN ECUMENICAL COUNCIL, Pastoral Constitution on the Church in the Modern World, *Gaudium et Spes*, 7 December 1965, 11.
[11] *Amoris Laetitia*, 56.

7. Against this background, the Congregation for Catholic Education has seen fit to offer this text to all who have a special interest in education, and to those whose work is touched by the question of gender theory. It is intended for the educational community involved in Catholic schools, and for all who, animated by the Christian vision of life, work in other types of school. The document is offered for use by parents, students, school leaders and personnel, bishops, priests, religious, ecclesial movements, associations of the lay faithful, and other relevant bodies.

# LISTENING

## BRIEF OVERVIEW

8. The primary outlook needed for anyone who wishes to take part in *dialogue* is *listening*. It is necessary, above all, to listen carefully to and understand cultural events of recent decades. The twentieth century brought new anthropological theories and with them the beginnings of gender theory. These were based on a reading of sexual differentiation that was strictly sociological, relying on a strong emphasis on the freedom of the individual. In fact, around the middle of the last century, a whole series of studies were published which accentuated time and again the role of external conditioning, including its influence on determining personality. When such studies were applied to human sexuality, they often did so with a view to demonstrating that sexuality identity was more a social construct than a given natural or biological fact.

9. These schools of thought were united in denying the existence of any original given element in the individual, which would precede and at the same time constitute our personal identity, forming the necessary basis of everything we do. According to such theories, the only thing that matters in personal relationships is the affection between the individuals involved, irrespective of sexual difference or procreation which would be seen as irrelevant in the formation of families. Thus, the institutional model of the family (where a structure and finality exist independent of the subjective preferences of the spouses) is bypassed, in favour of a vision of family that is purely contractual and voluntary.

10. Over the course of time, gender theory has expanded its field of application. At the beginning of the 1990s, its focus was upon the possibility of the individual determining his or her own sexual tendencies without having to take account of the reciprocity and complementarity of male-female relationships, nor of the

procreative end of sexuality. Furthermore, it was suggested that one could uphold the theory of a radical separation between gender and sex, with the former having priority over the latter. Such a goal was seen as an important stage in the evolution of humanity, in which "a society without sexual differences" could be envisaged.[12]

11. In this *cultural context*, it is clear that *sex* and *gender* are no longer synonyms or interchangeable concepts, since they are used to describe two different realities. Sex is seen as defining which of the two biological categories (deriving from the original feminine-masculine dyad) one belonged to. Gender, on the other hand, would be the way in which the differences between the sexes are lived in each culture. The problem here does not lie in the distinction between the two terms, which can be interpreted correctly, but in *the separation of sex from gender*. This separation is at the root of the distinctions proposed between various "sexual orientations" which are no longer defined by the sexual difference between male and female, and can then assume other forms, determined solely by the individual, who is seen as radically autonomous. Further, the concept of gender is seen as dependent upon the subjective mindset of each person, who can choose a gender not corresponding to his or her biological sex, and therefore with the way others see that person (*transgenderism*).

12. In a growing contraposition between nature and culture, the propositions of gender theory converge in the concept of "queer", which refers to dimensions of sexuality that are extremely fluid, flexible, and as it were, nomadic. This culminates in the assertion of the complete emancipation of the individual from any *a priori* given sexual definition, and the disappearance of classifications seen as overly rigid. This would create a new range of nuances that vary in degree and intensity according to both sexual orientation and the gender one has identified oneself with.

---

[12] *Idem.*

13. The duality in male-female couples is furthermore seen as in conflicting with the idea of "polyamory", that is, relationships involving more than two individuals. Because of this, it is claimed that the duration of relationships, as well as their binding nature, should be flexible, depending on the shifting desires of the individuals concerned. Naturally, this has consequences for the sharing of the responsibilities and obligations inherent in maternity and paternity. This new range of relationships become "kinship". These are: based upon desire or affection, often marked by a limited time span that is determined, ethically flexible, or even (sometimes by explicit mutual consent) without any hope of long-term meaning. What counts is the absolutely free self-determination of each individual and the choices he or she makes according to the circumstances of each relationship of affectivity.

14. This has led to calls for public recognition of the right to choose one's gender, and of a plurality of new types of unions, in direct contradiction of the model of marriage as being between one man and one woman, which is portrayed as a vestige of patriarchal societies. The ideal presented is that the individual should be able to choose his or her own status, and that society should limit itself to guaranteeing this right, and even providing material support, since the minorities involved would otherwise suffer negative social discrimination. The claim to such rights has become a regular part of political debate and has been included in documents at an international level, and in certain pieces of national legislation.

## POINTS OF AGREEMENT

15. From the whole field of writing on gender theory, there have however emerged some positions that could provide points of agreement, with a potential to yield growth in mutual understanding. For instance, educational programmes on this area often share a laudable desire to combat all expressions of

unjust discrimination, a requirement that can be shared by all sides. Such pedagogical material acknowledges that there have been delays and failings in this regard.[13] Indeed, it cannot be denied that through the centuries forms of unjust discrimination have been a sad fact of history and have also had an influence within the Church. This has brought a certain rigid *status quo*, delaying the necessary and progressive inculturation of the truth of Jesus's proclamation of the *equal dignity of men and women*, and has provoked accusations of a sort of masculinist mentality, veiled to a greater or lesser degree by religious motives.

16. Another position held in common is the need to educate children and young people *to respect every person* in their particularity and difference, so that no one should suffer bullying, violence, insults or unjust discrimination based on their specific characteristics (such as special needs, race, religion, sexual tendencies, etc.). Essentially, this involves educating for active and responsible citizenship, which is marked by the ability to welcome all legitimate expressions of human personhood with respect.

17. A further positive development in anthropological understanding also present in writing on gender has centred on *the values of femininity*. For example, women's "capacity for the other" favours a more realistic and mature reading of evolving situations, so that "a sense and a respect for what is concrete develop in her, opposed to abstractions which are so often fatal for the existence of individuals and society".[14] This is a contribution that enriches human relationships and spiritual values "beginning with daily relationships between people". Because of this, society owes a significant debt to the many women "who are involved

---

[13] Cf. FRANCIS, *Address to the Participants in the General Assembly of the Members of the Pontifical Academy for Life*, 5 October 2017.

[14] CONGREGATION FOR THE DOCTRINE OF THE FAITH, *Letter to Bishops of the Catholic Church on the Collaboration of Men and Women in the Church and in the World*, 31 May 2004, 13.

in the various *areas of education* extending well beyond the family: nurseries, schools, universities, social service agencies, parishes, associations and movements".[15]

18. Women have a unique understanding of reality. They possess a capacity to endure adversity and "to keep life going even in extreme situations" and hold on "tenaciously to the future".[16] This helps explain why "wherever the work of education is called for, we can note that women are ever ready and willing to give themselves generously to others, especially in serving the weakest and most defenceless. In this work they exhibit a kind of *affective, cultural and spiritual motherhood* which has inestimable value for the development of individuals and the future of society. At this point, how can I fail to mention the witness of so many Catholic women and Religious Congregations of women from every continent who have made education, particularly the education of boys and girls, their principal apostolate?".[17]

## CRITIQUE

19. Nonetheless, real life situations present gender theory with some valid *points of criticism*. Gender theory (especially in its most radical forms) speaks of a gradual process of denaturalisation, that is a move away from *nature* and towards an absolute option for the decision of the feelings of the human subject. In this understanding of things, the view of both sexuality identity and the family become subject to the same "liquidity" and "fluidity" that characterise other aspects of post-modern culture, often founded on nothing more than a confused concept of freedom in the realm of feelings and wants, or momentary desires provoked by emotional impulses and the will of the individual, as opposed to anything based on the truths of existence.

---

[15] JOHN PAUL II, *Letter to Women*, 29 June 1995, 9.

[16] CONGREGATION FOR THE DOCTRINE OF THE FAITH, *Letter to Bishops*, 13.

[17] JOHN PAUL II, *Letter to Women*, 9.

20. The underlying presuppositions of these theories can be traced back to a *dualistic anthropology*, separating body (reduced to the status of inert matter) from human will, which itself becomes an absolute that can manipulate the body as it pleases. This combination of physicalism and voluntarism gives rise to relativism, in which everything that exists is of equal value and at the same time undifferentiated, without any real order or purpose. In all such theories, from the most moderate to the most radical, there is agreement that one's gender ends up being viewed as more important than being of male or female sex. The effect of this move is chiefly to create a cultural and ideological revolution driven by relativism, and secondarily a juridical revolution, since such beliefs claim specific rights for the individual and across society.

21. In practice, the advocacy for the different identities often presents them as being of completely *equal value* compared to each other. This, however, actually negates the relevance of each one. This has particular importance for the question of sexual difference. In fact, the generic concept of "non-discrimination" often hides an ideology that denies the difference as well as natural reciprocity that exists between men and women. "Instead of combating wrongful interpretations of sexual difference that would diminish the fundamental importance of that difference for human dignity, such a proposal would simply eliminate it by proposing procedures and practices that make it irrelevant for a person's development and for human relationships. But the utopia of the 'neuter' eliminates both human dignity in sexual distinctiveness and the personal nature of the generation of new life".[18] The anthropological basis of the concept of family is thus emptied of meaning.

---

[18] FRANCIS, *Address to the Participants in the General Assembly of the Members of the Pontifical Academy for Life,* 5 October 2017, 3.

22. This ideology inspires educational programmes and legislative trends that promote ideas of personal identity and affective intimacy that make a radical break with the actual *biological difference* between male and female. Human identity is consigned to the individual's choice, which can also change in time. These ideas are the expression of a widespread way of thinking and acting in today's culture that confuses "genuine freedom with the idea that each individual can act arbitrarily as if there were no truths, values and principles to provide guidance, and everything were possible and permissible".[19]

23. The Second Vatican Council, wishing to express the Church's view of the human person, stated that "though made of body and soul, man is one. Through his bodily composition he gathers to himself the elements of the material world; thus they reach their crown through him, and through him raise their voice in free praise of the Creator".[20] Because of this dignity, "man is not wrong when he regards himself as superior to bodily concerns, and as more than a speck of nature or a nameless constituent of the city of man".[21] Therefore, "the expressions 'the order of nature' and 'the order of biology' must not be confused or regarded as identical, the 'biological order' does indeed mean the same as the order of nature but only in so far as this is accessible to methods of empirical and descriptive natural science, and not as a specific order of existence, with an obvious relationship to the First Cause, to God the Creator God".[22]

---

[19] *Amoris Laetitia*, 34.
[20] *Gaudium et Spes*, 14.
[21] *Idem*.
[22] K. Wojtyła, *Love and Responsibility*, London 1981, pp.56-57.

# REASONING

## RATIONAL ARGUMENTS

24. Taking into account our historical overview, together with certain points of agreement identified, and the critique that has been made of gender theory, we can now move to some considerations on the issue based on the light of reason. In fact, there are rational arguments to support the *centrality of the body* as an integrating element of personal identity and family relationships. The body is subjectivity that communicates identity of being.[23] In the light of this reality, we can understand why the data of biological and medical science shows that "sexual dimorphism" (that is, the sexual difference between men and women) can be demonstrated scientifically by such fields as genetics, endocrinology and neurology. From the point of view of genetics, male cells (which contain XY chromosomes) differ, from the very moment of conception, from female cells (with their XX chromosomes). That said, in cases where a person's sex is not clearly defined, it is medical professionals who can make a therapeutic intervention. In such situations, parents cannot make an arbitrary choice on the issue, let alone society. Instead, *medical science* should act with purely therapeutic ends, and intervene in the least invasive fashion, on the basis of objective parameters and with a view to establishing the person's constitutive identity.

25. The *process of identifying sexual identity* is made more difficult by the fictitious construct known as "gender neuter" or "third gender", which has the effect of obscuring the fact that a person's sex is a structural determinant of male or female identity. Efforts to go beyond the constitutive male-female sexual difference, such as the ideas of "intersex" or "transgender", lead to a masculinity or femininity that is ambiguous, even though

---

[23] Cf. JOHN PAUL II, Encyclical Letter *Veritatis Splendor*, 6 August 1993, 48.

(in a self-contradictory way), these concepts themselves actually presuppose the very sexual difference that they propose to negate or supersede. This oscillation between male and female becomes, at the end of the day, only a "provocative" display against so-called "traditional frameworks", and one which, in fact, ignores the suffering of those who have to live situations of sexual indeterminacy. Similar theories aim to annihilate the concept of "nature", (that is, everything we have been given as a pre-existing foundation of our being and action in the world), while at the same time implicitly reaffirming its existence.

26. Philosophical analysis also demonstrates that *sexual difference* between male and female is constitutive of human identity. Greek and Roman thinkers posit *essence* as the aspect of being that transcends, brings together and harmonises male-female difference within the unity of the *human person*. Within the tradition of hermeneutical and phenomenological philosophy, both sexual distinction and complementarity are interpreted in symbolic and metaphorical terms. Sexual difference in relationships is seen as constitutive of personal identity, whether this be at the level of the horizontal (in the *dyad* "man-woman") or vertical (in the *triad* "man-woman-God"). This applies equally to interpersonal "I-You" male-female relationships and to family relationships (You-I-We).

27. The *formation of one's identity* is itself based on the principle of otherness, since it is precisely the direct encounter between another "you" *who is not me* that enables me to recognise the essence of the "I" who is me. Difference, in fact, is a condition of *all cognition*, including cognition of one's identity. In the family, knowledge of one's mother and father allows the child to construct his or her own sexual identity and difference. Psychoanalytic theory demonstrates the *tri-polar value* of child-parent relationships, showing that sexual identity can only fully emerge in the light of the synergetic comparison that sexual differentiation creates.

28. The physiological *complementarity* of male-female sexual difference assures the necessary conditions for procreation. In contrast, only recourse to reproductive technology can allow one of the partners in a relationship of two persons of the same sex to generate offspring, using "in vitro" fertilisation and a surrogate mother. However, the use of such technology is not a replacement for natural conception, since it involves the manipulation of human embryos, the fragmentation of parenthood, the instrumentalisation and/or commercialisation of the human body as well as the reduction of a baby to an object in the hands of science and technology.[24]

29. In so far as this issue relates to the world of education, it is clear that by its very nature, education can help lay the foundations for peaceful dialogue and facilitate a fruitful meeting together of peoples and a meeting of minds. Further, it would seem that the prospect of a broadening of reason to include the *dimension of the transcendent* is not of secondary importance. The dialogue between Faith and Reason, "if it does not want to be reduced to a sterile intellectual exercise,... must begin from the present concrete situation of humanity and upon this develop a reflection that draws from the ontological-metaphysical truth".[25] The evangelising mission of the Church to men and women is carried out within this horizon.

---

[24] Cf. CONGREGATION FOR THE DOCTRINE OF THE FAITH, Instruction on Respect for Human Life in its Origin and the Dignity of Procreation, *Donum Vitae*, 22 February 1987, 4.

[25] BENEDICT XVI, *Address to the Participants of the sixth European Symposium of University Professors,* Rome, 7 June 2008.

# PROPOSING

## CHRISTIAN ANTHROPOLOGY

30. The Church, mother and teacher, does more than simply listen. Remaining rooted in her original mission, and at the same time always open to the contribution of reason, she puts herself at the service of the community of peoples, offering it a way of living. It is clear that if we are to provide well-structured educational programmes that are coherent with the true nature of human persons (with a view to guiding them towards a full actualisation of their sexual identity within the context of the vocation of self-giving), it is not possible to achieve this without a clear and convincing *anthropology* that gives a meaningful foundation to sexuality and affectivity. The first step in this process of throwing light on anthropology consists in recognising that "man too has a nature that he must respect and that he cannot manipulate at will".[26] This is the fulcrum on which to support a human ecology that moves from the "respect for our dignity as human beings" and from the necessary relationship of our life to "moral law, which is inscribed into our nature".[27]

31. Christian anthropology has its roots in the narrative of human origins that appears in the Book of Genesis, where we read that "God created man in his own image [...] male and female he created them." (*Gn* 1,27) These words capture not only the essence of the story of creation but also that of the life-giving relationship between men and women, which brings them into intimate union with God. The *self* is completed by the one who is *other than the self*, according to the specific identity of each person, and both have a point of encounter forming a dynamic of reciprocity which is derived from and sustained by the Creator.

---

[26] BENEDICT XVI, *Address at the Reichstag Building, Berlin*, 22 September 2011.

[27] FRANCIS, Encyclical Letter on Care for Our Common Home *Laudato Si'*, 24 May 2015, 154-155.

32. The Holy Scripture reveals the wisdom of the Creator's design, which "has assigned as a task to man his body, his masculinity and femininity; and that in masculinity and femininity he, in a way, assigned to him as a task his humanity, the dignity of the person, and also the clear sign of the interpersonal communion in which man fulfils himself through the authentic gift of himself".[28] Thus, *human nature* must be understood on the basis of the *unity of body and soul*, far removed from any sort of physicalism or naturalism, since "in the unity of his spiritual and biological inclinations and of all the other specific characteristics necessary for the pursuit of his end".[29]

33. This "unified totality"[30] integrates the vertical dimension (human communion with God) with the horizontal dimension constituted by the interpersonal communion that men and woman are called to live.[31] One's identity as a human person comes to authentic maturity to the extent that one opens up to others, for the very reason that "the configuration of our own mode of being, whether as male or female, is not simply the result of biological or genetic factors, but of multiple elements having to do with temperament, family history, culture, experience, education, the influence of friends, family members and respected persons, as well as other formative situations".[32] In reality, "the essential fact is that the human person becomes himself only with the other. The 'I' becomes itself only from the 'thou' and from the

---

[28] JOHN PAUL II, *General Audience,* 8 April 1981 in *Insegnamenti,* IV/1 (1981), p. 904.

[29] *Veritatis Splendor,* 50.

[30] Cf. *Idem.*

[31] "Man and woman constitute two modes of realising, on the part of the human creature, a determined participation in the Divine Being: they are created in the 'image and likeness of God' and they fully accomplish such vocation not only as single persons, but also as couples, which are communities of love. Oriented to unity and fecundity, the married man and woman participate in the creative love of God, living in communion with him through the other." *Educational Guidance in Human Love: Outlines for Sex Education,* 26. See also CONGREGATION FOR CATHOLIC EDUCATION, *Educating to Intercultural Dialogue in Catholic Schools: Living in Harmony for a Civilisation of Love,* 28 October 2013, 35-36.

[32] *Amoris Laetitia,* 286.

'you'. It is created for dialogue, for synchronic and diachronic communion. It is only the encounter with the 'you' and with the 'we' that the 'I' opens to itself ".[33]

34. There is a need to reaffirm the metaphysical roots of sexual difference, as an anthropological refutation of attempts to negate the male-female duality of human nature, from which the family is generated. The denial of this duality not only erases the vision of human beings as the fruit of an act of creation but creates the idea of the human person as a sort of abstraction who "chooses for himself what his nature is to be. Man and woman in their created state as complementary versions of what it means to be human are disputed. But if there is no pre-ordained duality of man and woman in creation, then neither is the family any longer a reality established by creation. Likewise, the child has lost the place he had occupied hitherto and the dignity pertaining to him".[34]

35. Seen from this perspective, education on sexuality and affectivity must involve each person in a process of learning "with perseverance and consistency, the meaning of his or her body"[35] in the full original truth of masculinity and femininity. It means "learning to accept our body, to care for it and to respect its fullest meaning [...] Also, valuing one's own body in its femininity or masculinity is necessary if I am going to be able to recognise myself in an encounter with someone who is different [...] and find mutual enrichment".[36] Therefore, in the light of a *fully human and integral ecology*, women and men will understand the real meaning of sexuality and genitality in terms of the intrinsically relational and communicative intentionality that both informs their bodily nature and moves each one towards the other mutually.

---

[33] BENEDICT XVI, *Address to the General Assembly of the Italian Episcopal Conference*, 27 May 2010.

[34] BENEDICT XVI, *Address to the Roman Curia*, 21 December 2012.

[35] *Amoris Laetitia*, 151.

[36] *Laudato Si'*, 155.

## THE FAMILY

36. The family is the natural place for the relationship of reciprocity and communion between man and woman to find its fullest realisation. For it is in the family that man and woman, united by a free and fully conscious *pact of conjugal love*, can live out "a totality in which all the elements of the person enter appeal of the body and instinct, power of feeling and affectivity, aspiration of the spirit and of will".[37] The family is "an anthropological fact, and consequently a social, cultural fact". On the other hand, to "qualify it with ideological concepts which are compelling at only one moment in history, and then decline"[38] would mean a betrayal of its true significance. The family, seen as a natural social unit which favours the maximum realisation of the reciprocity and complementarity between men and women, precedes even the socio-political order of the State whose legislative freedom must take it into account and give it proper recognition.

37. Reason tells us that two fundamental rights, which stem from the very nature of the family, must always be guaranteed and protected. Firstly, the family's right to be recognised as the primary pedagogical environment for the educational formation of children. This "primary right" finds its most concrete expression in the "most grave duty"[39] of parents to take responsibility for the "well-rounded personal and social education of their children",[40] including their sexual and affective education, "within the broader framework of an education for love, for mutual self-giving"[41]. This is at once an *educational right and responsibility* that is

---

[37] CATECHISM OF THE CATHOLIC CHURCH, 1643

[38] FRANCIS, *Address to Participants in the International Colloquium on the Complementarity Between Men and Women Sponsored by the Congregation for the Doctrine of the Faith*, 17 November 2014, 3.

[39] *Code of Canon Law*, can. 1136; cf. *Code of Canons of the Oriental Churches*, can. 627.

[40] *Gravissimum Educationis*, 3.

[41] *Amoris Laetitia*, 280

"essential, since it is connected with the transmission of human life; it is original and primary with regard to the educational role of others, on account of the uniqueness of the loving relationship between parents and children; and it is irreplaceable and inalienable, and therefore incapable of being entirely delegated to others or usurped by others".[42]

38. Children enjoy another right which is of equal importance: to "grow up in a family with a father and a mother capable of creating a suitable environment for the child's development and emotional maturity" and "continuing to grow up and mature in a correct relationship represented by the masculinity and femininity of a father and a mother and thus preparing for affective maturity".[43] It is precisely within the *nucleus of the family unit* that children can learn how to recognise the value and the beauty of the differences between the two sexes, along with their equal dignity, and their reciprocity at a biological, functional, psychological and social level. "Faced with a culture that largely reduces human sexuality to the level of something commonplace, since it interprets and lives it in a reductive and impoverished way by linking it solely with the body and with selfish pleasure, the educational service of parents must aim firmly at a training in the area of sex that is truly and fully personal: for sexuality is an enrichment of the whole person body, emotions and soul and it manifests its inmost meaning in leading the person to the gift of self in love".[44] Of course, such rights exist hand in hand with all the other fundamental rights of the human person, especially those concerning freedom of thought, conscience and religion. Wherever such things are held in common, those involved in education can find room for collaboration that is fruitful for all.

---

[42] *Familiaris Consortio*, 36.

[43] FRANCIS, *Address to Members of the Delegation of the International Catholic Child Bureau*, 11 April 2014.

[44] *Familiaris Consortio*, 37.

## THE SCHOOL

39. The primacy of the family in educating children is supplemented by the subsidiary role of schools. Strengthened by its roots in the Gospel, "The Catholic school sets out to be a school for the human person and of human persons. 'The person of each individual human being, in his or her material and spiritual needs, is at the heart of Christ's teaching: this is why the promotion of the human person is the goal of the Catholic school'. This affirmation, stressing man's vital relationship with Christ, reminds us that it is in his person that the fullness of the truth concerning man is to be found. For this reason the Catholic school, in committing itself to the development of the whole man, does so in obedience to the solicitude of the Church, in the awareness that all human values find their fulfilment and unity in Christ. This awareness expresses the centrality of the human person in the educational project of the Catholic school".[45]

40. The Catholic school should be an educating community in which the human person can express themselves and grow in his or her humanity, in a process of relational dialogue, interacting in a constructive way, exercising tolerance, understanding different points of view and creating trust in an atmosphere of authentic harmony. Such a school is truly an *"educating community, a place of differences living together in harmony.* The school community is a place for encounter and promoting participation. It dialogues with the family, which is the primary community to which the students that attend school belong. The school must respect the family's culture. It must listen carefully to the needs that it finds and the expectations that are directed towards it".[46] In this way, girls and boys are accompanied by a community that

---

[45] CONGREGATION FOR CATHOLIC EDUCATION, *The Catholic School on the Threshold of the Third Millennium*, 28 December 1997, 9.
[46] *Educating to Intercultural Dialogue in Catholic Schools*, 58.

teaches them "to overcome their individualism and discover, in the light of faith, their specific vocation to live responsibly in a community with others".[47]

41. Christians who live out their vocation to educate in schools which are not Catholic can also offer witness to, serve, and promote the truth about the human person. In fact, "the integral formation of the human person, which is the purpose of education, includes the development of all the human faculties of the students, together with preparation for professional life, formation of ethical and social awareness, becoming aware of the transcendental, and religious education".[48] *Personal witness*, when joined with professionalism, contributes greatly to the achievement of these objectives.

42. *Education in affectivity* requires language that is appropriate as well as measured. It must above all take into account that, while children and young people have not yet reached full maturity, they are preparing with great interest to experience all aspects of life. Therefore, it is necessary to help students "to develop a critical sense in dealing with the onslaught of new ideas and suggestions, the flood of pornography and the overload of stimuli that can deform sexuality".[49] In the face of a continuous bombardment of messages that are ambiguous and unclear, and which end up creating emotional disorientation as well as impeding psycho-relational maturity, young people "should be helped to recognise and seek out positive influences, while shunning the things that cripple their capacity for love".[50]

---

[47] CONGREGATION FOR CATHOLIC EDUCATION, *The Catholic School*, 19 March 1977, 45.

[48] CONGREGATION FOR CATHOLIC EDUCATION, *Lay Catholics in School: Witnesses to Faith*, 15 October 1982, 17.

[49] *Amoris Laetitia*, 281.

[50] *Idem.*

## SOCIETY

43. An overall perspective on the situation of contemporary society must form a part of the educational process. The *transformation of social and interpersonal relationships* "has often waved 'the flag of freedom', but it has, in reality, brought spiritual and material devastation to countless human beings, especially the poorest and most vulnerable. It is ever more evident that the decline of the culture of marriage is associated with increased poverty and a host of other social ills that disproportionately affect women, children and the elderly. It is always they who suffer the most in this crisis".[51]

44. In the light of all of this, the family must not be left to face the challenges of educating the young on its own. The Church, for its part, continues to support families and young people within communities that are open and welcoming. Schools and local communities are called, in particular, to carry out an important mission here, although they do not substitute the role of parents but complement it.[52] The notable urgency of the challenges faced by the work of human formation should act as stimulus towards reconstructing the *educational alliance between family, school and society.*

45. It is widely acknowledged that this educational alliance has entered into crisis. There is an urgent need to promote a new alliance that is genuine and not simply at the level of bureaucracy, a shared project that can offer a "positive and prudent sexual education"[53] that can harmonise the primary responsibility of parents with the work of teachers. We must create the right conditions for a constructive encounter between the various

---

[51] FRANCIS, *Address to Participants in the International Colloquium on the Complementarity Between Men and Women Sponsored by the Congregation for the Doctrine of the Faith,* 17 November 2014, 2.

[52] Cf. *Amoris Laetitia,* 84.

[53] *Gravissimum Educationis,* 1.

actors involved, making for an atmosphere of transparency where all parties constantly keep the others informed of what each is doing, facilitating maximum involvement and thus avoiding the unnecessary tensions that arise through misunderstandings caused by lack of clarity, information or competency.

46. Across this educational alliance, pedagogical activity should be informed by *the principle of subsidiarity*: "All other participants in the process of education are only able to carry out their responsibilities *in the name of the parents, with their consent* and, to a certain degree, *with their authorisation*".[54] If they succeed in working together, family, school and the broader society can produce educational programmes on affectivity and sexuality that respect each person's own stage of maturity regarding these areas and at the same time promote respect for the body of the other person. They would also take into account the physiological and psychological specificity of young people, as well as the phase of neurocognitive growth and maturity of each one, and thus be able to accompany them in their development in a healthy and responsible way.

## FORMING FORMATORS

47. All who work in human formation are called to exercise great responsibility in the work of effectively implementing the pedagogical projects in which they are involved. If they are people of personal maturity and balance who are well-prepared, this can have a strongly positive influence on students.[55] Therefore, it is important that their own formation includes not only professional qualifications but also cultural and spiritual preparedness. The *education of the human person*, especially developmentally, requires great care and ongoing formation. Simply repeating the

---

[54] JOHN PAUL II, Letter to Families *Gratissimam Sane*, 2 February 1994, 16; cf. PONTIFICAL COUNCIL FOR THE FAMILY, *Human Sexuality: Truth and Meaning. Educational Guidelines in the Family*, 8 December 1995, 23.

[55] Cf. *Educational Guidance in Human Love: Outlines for Sex Education*, 79.

standard points of a discipline is not enough. Today's educators are expected to be able "to accompany their students towards lofty and challenging goals, cherish high expectations for them, involve and connect students to each other and the world".[56]

48. School managers, teaching staff and personnel all share the responsibility of both guaranteeing delivery of a high-quality service coherent with the Christian principles that lie at the heart of their educational project, as well as interpreting the challenges of their time while giving the daily witness of their understanding, objectivity and prudence.[57] It is a commonly-accepted fact that "modern man listens more willingly to witnesses than to teachers, and if he does listen to teachers, it is because they are witnesses".[58] The *authority of an educator* is therefore built upon the concrete combination "of a general formation, founded on a positive and professional constructive concept of life, and of constant effort in realising it. Such a formation goes beyond the purely necessary professional training and addresses the more intimate aspects of the personality, including the religious and the spiritual".[59]

49. When the "formation of formators" is undertaken on the basis of Christian principles, it has as its objective not only the formation of individual teachers but the building up and consolidation of an entire *educational community* through a fruitful exchange between all involved, one that has both didactic and emotional dimensions. Thus, dynamic relationships grow between educators, and professional development is enriched by well-rounded personal growth, so that the work of

---

[56] CONGREGATION FOR CATHOLIC EDUCATION, *Educating Today and Tomorrow. A Renewing Passion,* Vatican City, 2014, Chapter II, 7.

[57] Cf. CONGREGATION FOR CATHOLIC EDUCATION, *Educating Together in the Catholic School. A Mission Shared by Consecrated Persons and the Lay Faithful,* 8 September 2007, 34-37.

[58] PAUL VI, Apostolic Exhortation *Evangelii Nuntiandi,* 8 December 1975, 41.

[59] *Educational Guidance in Human Love,* 80.

teaching is carried out at the service of humanisation. Therefore, Catholic educators need to be sufficiently prepared regarding the intricacies of the various questions that gender theory brings up and be fully informed about both current and proposed legislation in their respective jurisdictions, aided by persons who are qualified in this area, in a way that is balanced and dialogue-orientated. In addition, university-level institutes and centres of research are called to offer their own specific contribution here, so that adequate, up-to-date and life-long learning on this topic is always made available to educators.

50. Regarding the specific task of education in human love, undertaken "with the aid of the latest advances in psychology and the arts and science of teaching",[60] formators need to have "a suitable and serious psycho-pedagogic training which allows the seizing of particular situations which require a special solicitude".[61] As a consequence, "a clear vision of the situation is required because the method adopted not only gradually conditions the success of this delicate education, but also conditions cooperation between the various people in responsibility".[62]

51. The autonomy and freedom of teaching is recognised today in many legal systems. In such a context, schools can collaborate with Catholic institutes of higher education to develop a deepened understanding of the various aspects of education in sexuality, with the further aim of creating new teaching materials, pedagogic reference works and teaching manuals that are based on the "Christian vision of man and women".[63] To this end, pedagogues, those who work in teacher-training and experts on literature for children and adolescents alike can all contribute to

---

[60] *Gravissimum Educationis*, 1.
[61] *Educational Guidance in Human Love*, 81.
[62] *Ibid.*, 83.
[63] *Ibid.*, 22.

the creation of a body of innovative and creative tools that, in the face of other visions that are partial or distorted, offer a solid and integrated education of the human person from infancy onwards. Against the background of the renewal of the education alliance, collaboration at local, national and international level between all parties involved must not limit itself to sharing of ideas or useful swapping of best practice but should be made available as a key means of permanent formation of educators themselves.

# CONCLUSIONS

52. In conclusion, the *path of dialogue*, which involves listening, reasoning and proposing, appears the most effective way towards a positive transformation of concerns and misunderstandings, as well as a resource that in itself can help develop a network of relationships that is both more open and more human. In contrast, although ideologically-driven approaches to the delicate questions around gender proclaim their respect for diversity, they actually run the risk of viewing such difference as static realities and end up leaving them isolated and disconnected from each other.

53. The Christian educational proposal fosters deeper dialogue, true to its objective "to promote the realisation of man and woman through the development of all their being, incarnate spirits, and of the gifts of nature and of grace by which they are enriched by God".[64] This requires a sincere effort *to draw closer to the other* and it can be a natural antidote to the "throw-away" and isolation culture. In this way, we restate that "the original dignity of every man and woman is therefore inalienable and inaccessible to any power or ideology".[65]

54. Catholic educators are called to go beyond all ideological reductionism or homologising relativism by remaining faithful to their own gospel-based identity, in order *to transform positively the challenges of their times into opportunities* by following the path of listening, reasoning and proposing the Christian vision, while giving witness by their very presence, and by the consistency of their words and deeds[66]. Formators have the attractive educational mission to "teach them sensitivity

---

[64] *Educational Guidance in Human Love*, 21.

[65] FRANCIS, *Address to the Delegation from the 'Dignitatis Humanae' Institute*, 7 December 2013.

[66] Cf. *Educating to Intercultural Dialogue in Catholic Schools*, conclusion.

to different expressions of love, mutual concern and care, loving respect and deeply meaningful communication. All of these prepare them for an integral and generous gift of self that will be expressed, following a public commitment, in the gift of their bodies. Sexual union in marriage will thus appear as a sign of an all-inclusive commitment, enriched by everything that has preceded it".[67]

55. The culture of dialogue does not in any way contradict the legitimate aspirations of Catholic schools to maintain their own vision of human sexuality, in keeping with the right of families freely to base the education of their children upon *an integral anthropology*, capable of harmonising the human person's physical, psychic and spiritual identity. In fact, a democratic state cannot reduce the range of education on offer to a single school of thought, all the more so in relation to this extremely delicate subject, which is concerned on the one hand with the fundamentals of human nature, and on the other with natural rights of parents freely to choose any educational model that accords with the dignity of the human person. Therefore, every educational institute should provide itself with organisational structures and didactic programmes that ensure these parental rights are fully and concretely respected. If this is the case, the Christian pedagogy on offer will be able to provide a solid response to anthropologies characterised by fragmentation and provisionality.

56. The programmes dealing with formation in affectivity and sexuality offered by Catholic centres of education must take into consideration the age-group of the students being taught and treat each person with the maximum of respect. This can be achieved through a *way of accompanying* that is discreet and confidential, capable of reaching out to those who are experiencing complex and painful situations. Every school should therefore make sure

---

[67] *Amoris Laetitia*, 283.

it is an environment of trust, calmness and openness, particularly where there are cases that require time and careful discernment. It is essential that the right conditions are created to provide a patient and understanding ear, far removed from any unjust discrimination.

57. The Congregation for Catholic Education is well aware of the daily effort and unstinting care shown by those who work in schools and in the whole range of formal and informal pedagogic endeavour. The Congregation wishes to encourage them in their pursuit of the work of forming young people, especially those among them who are affected by any form of poverty, and those in need of the love shown them by their educators, so that, in the words of St John Bosco, young people are not only loved, but know they are loved. This Dicastery would also like to express its warmest gratitude to all Christians who teach in Catholic schools or other types of school, and, in the words of Pope Francis, encourages them "to stimulate in the pupils the openness to the other as a face, as a person, as a brother and sister to know and respect, with his or her history, merits and defects, riches and limits. The challenge is to cooperate to train young people to be open and interested in the reality that surrounds them, capable of care and tenderness".[68]

Vatican City, 2 February 2019,
*Feast of the Presentation of the Lord.*

**Giuseppe Cardinal Versaldi**
Prefect

**Archbishop Angelo Vincenzo Zani**
Secretary

---

[68] FRANCIS, *Address to the Italian Catholic Primary School Teachers Association*, 5 January 2018.